You Know You're a Teacher If . . .

by
Char Forsten, Jim Grant, and Betty Hollas

Illustrated by
Phyllis Pittet

*Many thanks to creative teachers like
Anne Cromwell-Gapp, Penny King, and Wendy Young
for their unique and practical strategy contributions to this book.*

Published by Crystal Springs Books • Peterborough, New Hampshire
1-800-321-0401

You Know You're a Teacher If . . .

. . . you convince your optometrist to donate old, lenseless glass frames for your students to use as special "reading" glasses.

LET'S READ

. . . you stand looking at PVC pipe at the hardware store, explaining to the helpful clerk, "I just want to make some phones."

. . . you frequent the grocery store to replenish your classroom's supply of rotten fruits and vegetables.

SCIENCE TIMES
OBSERVE
1. color
2. smell
3. texture
skin

. . . you realize those extra feet of new rain gutter
can be put to good use in your classroom.

I LOST
Tooth
The Little Duck
Cinderella
Puss 'n Boots
The Littlest Book
POETRY Through The Ages
HOW TO COUNT TO
100
POOF
LEAH'S PONY
Voyager

. . . you know that buying old metal cookie sheets at a yard sale doesn't necessarily mean you'll be doing any baking.

ĭt ăt ŏt ŭt
sit cat cot cut
fit not but
kit dot gut

. . . you check out the end-of-the-summer sales at your local department store in hopes of finding some inflatable beach balls you can write on.

Homework
Math
Geography
7 × 1 =
7 × 2 =
7 × 3 =
7 × 4 =
7 × 5 =
7 × 6 =
8 × 4 =
8 × 5 =
8 × 6 =
8 × 7 =
8 × 8 =
8 × 9 =

. . . you recover from discovering your cat has chewed your new Venetian blind, because you know just what you can do with those damaged slats.

January
S M T W Th F S
1 2 3 4 5
6 7 8 9 10 11 12
1 + 3 =
5 4 7
7

. . . you uncover a chair in your attic and realize that, with a little painting, it could be transformed into something very special.

Author's Chair

. . . you unfold the USA material at the fabric store and finally understand how you can create that geography center.

MAP OF THE WORLD

. . . you spend quality time with your husband by cutting then edging shower board with colorful electrical tape for student white boards.

WRITING
CENTER
SOX
BOX

. . . you ask the owner of the local pizzeria for 25 cardboard pizza rounds and some menus.

LORENZO'S
PIZZERIA
IF YOU GAVE THE SALESCLE
A $20 BILL, WHAT WILL
YOUR CHANGE BE?
2 sodas 3.50
2 pizza slices 4.35

. . . you turn painters' tape into "Boo-Boo" tape so your students can cover and correct the errors you find on chart paper.

BOO-BOO TAPE
Today is Tuesday,
March 3, 2000. This
mor
our class
the
Homework

. . . you *want* those rings on the chickens' legs at the poultry farm.

Book Binding Station
• chicken rings
• pipe cleaners
• paper
• paper punch

. . . you find yourself more interested in buying something for its container than for its contents.

magic markers
Chocolate
Dice
with ridges
Unifix Cubes
Kool Whip
Counting
Beans

. . . you make “curriculum caps” out of painters’ caps for your students by adding big, wiggly eyes, fuzzy noses, and pipe-cleaner antennae.

DON'T BUG ME! I'M READING
DONT BUG ME! I'M WRITING
DONT BUG ME! I'm DOING MATH.

And you know you're a teacher if a room full of smiling faces makes those early mornings, late nights, and busy days all worthwhile.